Real People

J. K. Rowling

By Mary Hill

Welcome Books™

Children's Press®
A Division of Scholastic Inc.
New York / Toronto / London / Auckland / Sydney
Mexico City / New Delhi / Hong Kong
Danbury, Connecticut

Photo Credits: Cover © MC PHERSON COLIN/Corbis Sygma; p. 5, 21 © Reuters NewMedia Inc./TimePix; pp. 7, 9 photos courtesy of University of Exeter, England; pp. 11, 15, 17, 19 © AP/Wide World Photos; p.13 © Scott Laparruque/TimePix
Contributing Editor: Jennifer Silate
Book Design: Daniel Hosek

Library of Congress Cataloging-in-Publication Data

Hill, Mary, 1977-
  J. K. Rowling / by Mary Hill.
  p. cm.
  Includes index.
  Summary: Photographs and simple text introduce J. K. Rowling, author of the best-selling Harry Potter novels.
  ISBN 0-516-25866-4 (lib. bdg.)—ISBN 0-516-27888-6 (pbk.)
  1. Rowling, J. K.—Juvenile literature. 2. Authors, English—20th century—Biography—Juvenile literature. 3. Potter, Harry (Fictitious character)—Juvenile literature. 4. Children's stories—Authorship—Juvenile literature. [1. Rowling, J. K. 2. Authors, English. 3. Women—Biography.] I. Title.

PR6068.O93Z7323 2003
823'.914—dc21

                                                    2002156463

Contents

Meet J. K. Rowling.

She is a **writer**.

5

J. K. Rowling was born in **England**.

7

She went to **college** in England, too.

9

J. K. Rowling writes books for children.

11

She writes books about a boy named Harry Potter.

Harry Potter is studying to be a **wizard**.

THE EXTRAORDINARY NEW YORK TIMES BESTSELLER

Harry Potter
AND THE
SORCERER'S STONE

J. K. ROWLING

THE PHENOMENAL NATIONAL BESTSELLER

Harry Potter
AND THE
CHAMBER OF SECRETS

J. K. ROWLING

Harry Potter books are very **popular**.

Many children around the world like to read them.

15

Adults also read J. K. Rowling's books.

They like them, too.

J. K. Rowling gives **speeches**.

She talks to people about writing.

19

J. K. Rowling has won **awards** for her books.

She is a very good writer.

21

New Words

awards (uh-**wordz**) prizes given to a person for doing something well

college (**kol**-ij) a place of higher learning where students can continue to study after they have finished high school

England (**ing**-land) a country in Europe

popular (**pop**-yuh-lur) liked or enjoyed by many people

speeches (**speech**-uhz) talks given to groups of people

wizard (**wiz**-uhrd) a person, especially a man, believed to have magic powers

writer (**rite**-uhr) someone who writes

To Find Out More

Books
Conversations with J. K. Rowling
by J. K. Rowling and Lindsey Fraser
Scholastic

Harry Potter and the Sorceror's Stone
by J. K. Rowling
Scholastic

Web Site
The Magical World of Harry Potter
http://library.thinkquest.org/J001330/?tqskip1=1&tqtime=1108
Read about J. K. Rowling and Harry Potter and play Harry Potter
games on this Web site.

Index

About the Author
Mary Hill writes and edits children's books.

Reading Consultants
Kris Flynn, Coordinator, Small School District Literacy, The San Diego County Office of Education

Shelly Forys, Certified Reading Recovery Specialist, W.J. Zahnow Elementary School, Waterloo, IL

Sue McAdams, Former President of the North Texas Reading Council of the IRA, and Early Literacy Consultant, Dallas, TX